Great Works

Instructional Guides for Literature

The Westing Game

A guide for the novel by Ellen Raskin
Great Works Author: Jessica Case, M.A.Ed.

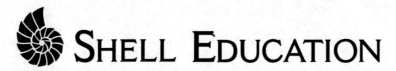

SHELL EDUCATION

Publishing Credits

Corinne Burton, M.A.Ed., *Publisher*; Emily R. Smith, M.A.Ed., *Content Director*; Lee Aucoin, *Senior Graphic Designer*; Brenda Van Dixhorn, *Editor*; Stephanie Bernard, *Associate Editor*; Jess Johnson, *Graphic Designer*

Image Credits

Front cover (all) iStock

Standards

© 2007 Teachers of English to Speakers of Other Languages, Inc. (TESOL)

© 2012 Board of Regents of the University of Wisconsin System, on behalf of WIDA—www.wida.us

© Copyright 2010. National Governors Association Center for Best Practices and Council of Chief State School Officers. All rights reserved.

ISTE Standards for Students, ©2016, ISTE® (International Society for Technology in Education), iste.org. All rights reserved.

© Copyright 2007–2018 Texas Education Association (TEA). All rights reserved.

Shell Education

A division of Teacher Created Materials

5301 Oceanus Drive

Huntington Beach, CA 92649-1030

www.tcmpub.com/shell-education

ISBN 978-1-4807-8518-2

© 2018 Shell Educational Publishing, Inc.

Table of Contents

How to Use This Literature Guide

Today's standards demand rigor and relevance in the reading of complex texts. The units in this series guide teachers in a rich and deep exploration of worthwhile works of literature for classroom study. The most rigorous instruction can also be interesting and engaging!

Many current strategies for effective literacy instruction have been incorporated into these instructional guides for literature. Throughout the units, text-dependent questions are used to determine comprehension of the book as well as student interpretation of the vocabulary words. The books chosen for the series are complex exemplars of carefully crafted works of literature. Close reading is used throughout the units to guide students toward revisiting the text and using textual evidence to respond to prompts orally and in writing. Students must analyze the story elements in multiple assignments for each section of the book. All of these strategies work together to rigorously guide students through their study of literature.

The next few pages will make clear how to use this guide for a purposeful and meaningful literature study. Each section of this guide is set up in the same way to make it easier for you to implement the instruction in your classroom.

Theme Thoughts

The great works of literature used throughout this series have important themes that have been relevant to people for many years. Many of the themes will be discussed during the various sections of this instructional guide. However, it would also benefit students to have independent time to think about the key themes of the novel.

Before students begin reading, have them complete *Pre-Reading Theme Thoughts* (page 13). This graphic organizer will allow students to think about the themes outside the context of the story. They'll have the opportunity to evaluate statements based on important themes and defend their opinions. Be sure to have students keep their papers for comparison to the *Post-Reading Theme Thoughts* (page 64). This graphic organizer is similar to the pre-reading activity. However, this time, students will be answering the questions from the point of view of one of the characters in the novel. They have to think about how the character would feel about each statement and defend their thoughts. To conclude the activity, have students compare what they thought about the themes before they read the novel to what the characters discovered during the story.

How to Use This Literature Guide (cont.)

Vocabulary

Each teacher overview page has definitions and sentences about how key vocabulary words are used in the section. These words should be introduced and discussed with students. There are two student vocabulary activity pages in each section. On the first page, students are asked to define the ten words chosen by the author of this unit. On the second page in most sections, each student will select at least eight words that he or she finds interesting or difficult. For each section, choose one of these pages for your students to complete. With either assignment, you may want to have students get into pairs to discuss the meanings of the words. Allow students to use reference guides to define the words. Monitor students to make sure the definitions they have found are accurate and relate to how the words are used in the text.

On some of the vocabulary student pages, students are asked to answer text-related questions about the vocabulary words. The following question stems will help you create your own vocabulary questions if you'd like to extend the discussion.

- How does this word describe _____'s character?
- In what ways does this word relate to the problem in this story?
- How does this word help you understand the setting?
- In what ways is this word related to the story's solution?
- Describe how this word supports the novel's theme of . . . .
- What visual images does this word bring to your mind?
- For what reasons might the author have chosen to use this particular word?

At times, more work with the words will help students understand their meanings. The following quick vocabulary activities are a good way to further study the words.

- Have students practice their vocabulary and writing skills by creating sentences and/or paragraphs in which multiple vocabulary words are used correctly and with evidence of understanding.
- Students can play vocabulary concentration. Students make a set of cards with the words and a separate set of cards with the definitions. Then, students lay the cards out on the table and play concentration. The goal of the game is to match vocabulary words with their definitions.
- Students can create word journal entries about the words. Students choose words they think are important and then describe why they think each word is important within the novel.

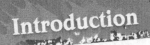

How to Use This Literature Guide (cont.)

Analyzing the Literature

After students have read each section, hold small-group or whole-class discussions. Questions are written at two levels of complexity to allow you to decide which questions best meet the needs of your students. The Level 1 questions are typically less abstract than the Level 2 questions. Level 1 is indicated by a square, while Level 2 is indicated by a triangle. These questions focus on the various story elements, such as character, setting, and plot. Student pages are provided if you want to assign these questions for individual student work before your group discussion. Be sure to add further questions as your students discuss what they've read. For each question, a few key points are provided for your reference as you discuss the novel with students.

Reader Response

In today's classrooms, there are often great readers who are below-average writers. So much time and energy is spent in classrooms getting students to read on grade level that little time is left to focus on writing skills. To help teachers include more writing in their daily literacy instruction, each section of this guide has a literature-based reader response prompt. Each of the three genres of writing is used in the reader responses within this guide: narrative, informative/explanatory, and opinion/argument. Students have a choice between two prompts for each reader response. One response requires students to make connections between the reading and their own lives. The other prompt requires students to determine text-to-text connections or connections within the text.

Close Reading the Literature

Within each section, students are asked to closely reread a short section of text. Since some versions of the novels have different page numbers, the selections are described by chapter and location, along with quotations to guide the readers. After each close reading, there are text-dependent questions to be answered by students.

Encourage students to read each question one at a time and then go back to the text and discover the answer. Work with students to ensure that they use the text to determine their answers rather than making unsupported inferences. Once students have answered the questions, discuss what they discovered. Suggested answers are provided in the answer key.

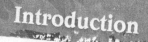

How to Use This Literature Guide (cont.)

Close Reading the Literature (cont.)

The generic, open-ended stems below can be used to write your own text-dependent questions if you would like to give students more practice.

- Give evidence from the text to support . . . .
- Justify your thinking using text evidence about . . . .
- Find evidence to support your conclusions about . . . .
- What text evidence helps the reader understand . . . ?
- Use the book to tell why _____ happens.
- Based on events in the story, ...
- Use text evidence to describe why . . . .

Making Connections

The activities in this section help students make cross-curricular connections to writing, mathematics, science, social studies, or the fine arts. Each of these types of activities requires higher-order thinking skills from students.

Creating with the Story Elements

It is important to spend time discussing the common story elements in literature. Understanding the characters, setting, and plot can increase students' comprehension and appreciation of the story. If teachers discuss these elements daily, students will more likely internalize the concepts and look for the elements in their independent reading. Another important reason for focusing on the story elements is that students will be better writers if they think about how the stories they read are constructed.

Students are given three options for working with the story elements. They are asked to create something related to the characters, setting, or plot of the novel. Students are given a choice in this activity so that they can decide to complete the activity that most appeals to them. Different multiple intelligences are used so that the activities are diverse and interesting to all students.

How to Use This Literature Guide (cont.)

Culminating Activity

This open-ended, cross-curricular activity requires higher-order thinking and allows for a creative product. Students will enjoy getting the chance to share what they have discovered through reading the novel. Be sure to allow them enough time to complete the activity at school or home.

Comprehension Assessment

The questions in this section are modeled after current standardized tests to help students analyze what they've read and prepare for tests they may see in their classrooms. The questions are dependent on the text and require critical-thinking skills to answer.

Response to Literature

The final post-reading activity is an essay based on the text that also requires further research by students. This is a great way to extend this book into other curricular areas. A suggested rubric is provided for teacher reference.

Correlation to the Standards

Shell Education is committed to producing educational materials that are research and standards based. As part of this effort, we have correlated all of our products to the academic standards of all 50 states, the District of Columbia, the Department of Defense Dependents Schools, and all Canadian provinces.

Purpose and Intent of Standards

The Every Student Succeeds Act (ESSA) mandates that all states adopt challenging academic standards that help students meet the goal of college and career readiness. While many states already adopted academic standards prior to ESSA, the act continues to hold states accountable for detailed and comprehensive standards. Standards are statements that describe the criteria necessary for students to meet specific academic goals. They define the knowledge, skills, and content students should acquire at each level. State standards are used in the development of our products, so educators can be assured they meet state academic requirements.

How to Find Standards Correlations

To print a customized correlation report of this product for your state, visit our website at **www.teachercreatedmaterials.com/administrators/correlations/** and follow the online directions. If you require assistance in printing correlation reports, please contact our Customer Service Department at 1-877-777-3450.

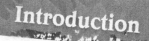

Correlation to the Standards (cont.)

Standards Correlation Chart

The lessons in this guide were written to support today's college and career readiness standards. This chart indicates which sections of this guide address which standards.

College and Career Readiness Standard	Section
Read closely to determine what the text says explicitly and to make logical inferences from it; cite specific textual evidence when writing or speaking to support conclusions drawn from the text.	Close Reading the Literature Sections 1–5; Making Connections Sections 2, 4; Creating with the Story Elements Sections 1–5; Culminating Activity
Determine central ideas or themes of a text and analyze their development; summarize the key supporting details and ideas.	Analyzing the Literature Sections 1–5; Creating with the Story Elements Section 5; Post-Reading Response to Literature
Analyze how and why individuals, events, or ideas develop and interact over the course of a text.	Analyzing the Literature Sections 1–5; Creating with the Story Elements Sections 2–3, 5
Interpret words and phrases as they are used in a text, including determining technical, connotative, and figurative meanings, and analyze how specific word choices shape meaning or tone.	Vocabulary Sections 1–5; Making Connections Section 1; Culminating Activity
Read and comprehend complex literary and informational texts independently and proficiently.	Reader Response Sections 1–5; Culminating Activity
Write arguments to support claims in an analysis of substantive topics or texts using valid reasoning and relevant and sufficient evidence.	Reader Response Sections 1–3; Post-Reading Response to Literature
Write informative/explanatory texts to examine and convey complex ideas and information clearly and accurately through the effective selection, organization, and analysis of content.	Reader Response Sections 1, 4–5; Making Connections Section 1
Write narratives to develop real or imagined experiences or events using effective technique, well-chosen details and well-structured event sequences.	Reader Response Sections 1–3, 5; Making Connections Section 3
Produce clear and coherent writing in which the development, organization, and style are appropriate to task, purpose, and audience.	Making Connections Sections 3–5; Post-Reading Response to Literature
Demonstrate command of the conventions of standard English grammar and usage when writing or speaking.	Analyzing the Literature Sections 1–5; Making Connections Sections 3–4

Correlation to the Standards (cont.)

Standards Correlation Chart (cont.)

College and Career Readiness Standard	Section
Determine or clarify the meaning of unknown and multiple-meaning words and phrases by using context clues, analyzing meaningful word parts, and consulting general and specialized reference materials, as appropriate.	Vocabulary Sections 1–5; Understanding Vocabulary Words Sections 1–5; During Reading Vocabulary Activity Sections 1–5
Acquire and use accurately a range of general academic and domain-specific words and phrases sufficient for reading, writing, speaking, and listening at the college and career readiness level; demonstrate independence in gathering vocabulary knowledge when encountering an unknown term important to comprehension or expression.	Vocabulary Sections 1–5; Understanding Vocabulary Words Sections 1–5; During Reading Vocabulary Activity Sections 1–5

TESOL and WIDA Standards

The lessons in this book promote English language development for English language learners. The following TESOL and WIDA English Language Development Standards are addressed through the activities in this book:

- Standard 1: English language learners communicate for social and instructional purposes within the school setting.
- Standard 2: English language learners communicate information, ideas and concepts necessary for academic success in the content area of language arts.

About the Author—Ellen Raskin

Ellen Raskin was born on March 13, 1928, in Milwaukee, Wisconsin. She grew up during the Great Depression, but that didn't stop her from having an enjoyable childhood. She loved to read, sing, and spend time with her family on the shore of Lake Michigan. Raskin went to the University of Wisconsin-Madison at the age of 17, where she originally majored in journalism; however, a visit to the Chicago Art Institute after her first year inspired Raskin to change her major to fine art.

After college, Raskin married, had a daughter named Susan, and eventually moved to New York City. In New York, she was hired at a commercial art studio where she prepared others' artwork for printing. During that time, she began to develop her own freelance career as a commercial artist. Raskin illustrated for several publishers and journals, including *The Saturday Evening Post*. She is credited with the design of over 1,000 book jackets and with the illustrations for more than a dozen children's books. After many years of illustrating for others, Raskin decided to create her own picture book, *Nothing Ever Happens on My Block*. As her independent career grew, Raskin gradually stopped doing commercial art and spent her time writing and illustrating her own children's books. Raskin's picture and chapter books usually contain problems to solve. Her works have been awarded over 20 literary awards, including the Newbery Medal for *The Westing Game*. Raskin's home and studio were located in a two-family house in Greenwich Village. She lived there with her husband, daughter, and son-in-law. Raskin died in 1984 from complications associated with a connective tissue disease.

Possible Texts for Text Comparisons

The Tattooed Potato and Other Clues is another great mystery by Ellen Raskin. Like *The Westing Game*, it has various plots, numerous characters, and keeps the reader guessing.

Raskin's other book, *The Mysterious Disappearance of Leon (I Mean Noel)*, is written in a style similar to *The Westing Game*. Clues are provided throughout the story to help solve the mystery of Leon's (I mean Noel's) disappearance.

Book Summary of *The Westing Game*

The reading of Samuel W. Westing's brings together 16 of the most unlikely people, who happen to reside in the Sunset Towers apartment building located on the shore of Lake Michigan. In order to find the true heir to Mr. Westing's fortune, they must play his game of "who-done-it." The 16 potential heirs are split into eight groups of two. Each pair is given a different set of clues and $10,000. Once the will is read and the clues distributed, interesting events unfold as they try to figure out who the real killer is. The players attempt to meet together on many occasions to learn more about each other's clues. At each meeting, however, something strange, interesting, or eye-opening occurs to twist the plot even more. As the game is played, details emerge about individual players and their pasts. Each player has a relationship with Sam Westing and possibly even a motive for his murder. Read and discover what the players learn and who is actually responsible for the death of Sam Westing.

Cross-Curricular Connection

This is a book of logic. The reader must be attentive to details and able to organize information from the text to solve the mystery. It would be a good book to use with reasoning, data collection, and logic lessons. This book can also be used during a social studies unit on the Midwest. Finally, this book is great for a genre study of mysteries.

Possible Texts for Text Sets

- Abrahams, Peter. 2006. *Down the Rabbit Hole (An Echo Falls Mystery)*. New York: HarperCollins.
- Balliett, Blue. 2005. *Chasing Vermeer*. New York: Scholastic.
- Konigsburg, E.L. 2007. *From the Mixed-up Files of Mrs. Basil E. Frankweiler*. New York: Atheneum Books for Young Readers.
- Snyder, Zilpha Keatley. 2006. *The Egypt Game*. New York: Atheneum Books for Young Readers.

Name _____

Date _____

Pre-Reading Theme Thoughts

Directions: Read each of the statements in the first column. Decide if you agree or disagree with the statements. Record your opinion by marking an *X* in Agree or Disagree for each statement. Explain your choices in the fourth column. There are no right or wrong answers.

Statement	Agree	Disagree	Explain Your Answer
Everything isn't always as it seems.			
A chain of events can blow you completely off course.			
Not all conclusions end the way you think they should.			
Sometimes the answer is right there in plain sight.			

Vocabulary Overview

Ten key words from this section are provided below with definitions and sentences about how the words are used in the book. Choose one of the vocabulary activity sheets (pages 15 or 16) for students to complete as they read this section. Monitor the students as they work to ensure the definitions they have found are accurate and relate to the text. Finally, discuss these important vocabulary words with the students. If you think these words or other words in the section warrant more time devoted to them, there are suggestions in the introduction for other vocabulary activities (page 5).

Word	Definition	Sentence about Text
tenants (ch. 1)	people who rent a place to live	Some **tenants** are more excited than others to rent apartments in Sunset Towers.
reupholstered (ch. 1)	provided furniture with another cover	Grace Windsor Wexler plans to have her furniture **reupholstered** her furniture before moving into Sunset Towers.
hassock (ch. 3)	a firm cushion, like a footstool	Angela Wexler stands on a **hassock** while she gets her wedding dress fitted.
craned (ch. 3)	stretched the neck so as to see better	Mrs. Wexler **cranes** her neck so she can see the smoke rising from the Westing house.
facade (ch. 3)	an outward appearance that does not truly reflect inner feelings	Crow's tough **facade** does not show the pain she feels as a corn is removed from her foot.
meager (ch. 4)	small in amount or quality	Sam Westing starts out with **meager** funds but soon grows his estate.
beneficiary (ch. 4)	the person who receives funds or other advantages	Otis Amber is named a **beneficiary** to Sam Westing's estate.
tottered (ch. 5)	moved without being stable, as if about to fall	Using a crutch to help her, Sydelle Pulaski **totters** over to the table.
eccentric (ch. 6)	acting in a very unusual or unexpected way	Sam Westing's **eccentric** will is puzzling for all who hear it read.
dastardly (ch. 6)	extremely wicked	The murder of Samuel Westing is a **dastardly** act.

Name _____

Date _____

Understanding Vocabulary Words

Directions: The following words appear in this section of the book. Use context clues and reference materials to determine an accurate definition for each word.

Word	Definition
tenants (ch. 1)	
reupholstered (ch. 1)	
hassock (ch. 3)	
craned (ch. 3)	
facade (ch. 3)	
meager (ch. 4)	
beneficiary (ch. 4)	
tottered (ch. 5)	
eccentric (ch. 6)	
dastardly (ch. 6)	

Name _____

Date _____

During-Reading Vocabulary Activity

Directions: As you read these chapters, record at least eight important words on the lines below. Try to find interesting, difficult, intriguing, special, or funny words. Your words can be long or short. They can be hard or easy to spell. After each word, use context clues in the text and reference materials to define the word.

- _____
- _____
- _____
- _____
- _____
- _____
- _____
- _____
- _____
- _____

Directions: Respond to these questions about the words in this section.

1. Explain why Crow is putting on a **facade**.

   _____

   _____

   _____

2. Give examples of how Sam Westing is **eccentric**.

   _____

   _____

   _____

Analyzing the Literature

Provided below are discussion questions you can use in small groups, with the whole class, or for written assignments. Each question is given at two levels so you can choose the right question for each group of students. Activity sheets with these questions are provided (pages 18–19) if you want students to write their responses. For each question, a few key discussion points are provided for your reference.

Story Element	■ Level 1	▲ Level 2	Key Discussion Points
Setting	Use details from the text to describe Sunset Towers.	How is Sunset Towers similar to or different from other apartment buildings?	Sunset Towers faces east and is on the shore of Lake Michigan. The building has many windows. People can see out the windows, but no one can see in. The businesses make it different from other apartments. Residents receive personal invitations to move in.
Character	Describe Angela and Turtle Wexler.	Compare and contrast Angela and Turtle Wexler.	Turtle is the youngest daughter of Grace and Jake Wexler. She is often overlooked and not appreciated. Turtle is a smart girl, always up for a dare or an adventure. Angela is the older daughter who is engaged to D. Denton Deere. She is extremely quiet and does as her mother says.
Character	Who is Sam Westing?	How is Sam Westing shown to play an important role in the early part of this story?	He founded the Westing Paper Products Corporation and Westingtown. His life was marked with sorrow; his daughter drowned, he was in a terrible accident, and he was sued by an inventor. His death brings together 16 possible heirs and suspects who work to determine who killed him.
Plot	What is the problem in this story?	Describe how the problem in this story relates to Sam Westing's eccentric life.	Sam Westing is found dead in his home and is said to have been murdered by one of the beneficiaries. Now that he is dead, Westing requires his heirs to play a game of "who-done-it."

Name _____

Date _____

Analyzing the Literature

Directions: Think about the section you just read. Read each question, and state your response with textual evidence.

1. Use details from the text to describe Sunset Towers.

   _____
   _____
   _____
   _____
   _____

2. Describe Angela and Turtle Wexler.

   _____
   _____
   _____
   _____
   _____

3. Who is Sam Westing?

   _____
   _____
   _____
   _____

4. What is the problem in this story?

   _____
   _____
   _____
   _____

Name _____

Date _____

▲ Analyzing the Literature

Directions: Think about the section you just read. Read each question, and state your response with textual evidence.

1. How is Sunset Towers similar to or different from other apartment buildings?

    _____

    _____

    _____

    _____

2. Compare and contrast Angela and Turtle Wexler.

    _____

    _____

    _____

    _____

3. How is Sam Westing shown to play an important role in the early part of this story?

    _____

    _____

    _____

    _____

4. Describe how the problem in this story relates to Sam Westing's eccentric life.

    _____

    _____

    _____

    _____

Name _____

Date _____

Reader Response

Directions: Choose one of the following prompts about this section to answer. Be sure you include a topic sentence in your response, use textual evidence to support your opinion, and provide a strong conclusion that summarizes your opinion.

Writing Prompts

- **Informative/Explanatory Piece**—What information does Sam Westing provide in his will? What do we learn about the people gathered to hear the will being read?
- **Narrative Piece**—The heirs in the story seem as though they will not get along well. What is some advice you can give them as they prepare to play the Westing Game?

_____

_____

_____

_____

_____

_____

_____

_____

_____

_____

_____

_____

_____

_____

_____

_____

_____

Name _____

Date _____

Close Reading the Literature

Directions: Closely reread the section in chapter 1 where Barney Northrup rents out all the apartments in one day. Start where Mrs. Wexler states, "Oh Jake, this apartment is perfect for us, just perfect." Continue reading to the end of chapter 1. Read each question, and then revisit the text to find evidence that supports your answer.

1. It seems that Sydelle Pulaski isn't as happy with Sunset Towers as some of the other tenants. Give specific examples from the text that support this.

   _____

   _____

   _____

2. What is the purpose of the last paragraph in chapter 1? What predictions can you make about the story based on this paragraph?

   _____

   _____

   _____

3. Barney Northrup is not a main character or even a real person. What is his role? Why do you think the author included him in the story? Who do you think he could be?

   _____

   _____

   _____

4. Use examples from the story to explain who seems to be in charge in the Wexler family.

   _____

   _____

   _____

Name _____

Date _____

Making Connections–Tenants of Sunset Towers

Directions: Six apartments have been leased in Sunset Towers. Use the graphic organizer below to arrange information about the tenants.

Apartment Number:	Apartment Number:
Tenants:	Tenants:
Information Known:	Information Known:

Apartment Number:	Apartment Number:
Tenants:	Tenants:
Information Known:	Information Known:

Apartment Number:	Apartment Number:
Tenants:	Tenants:
Information Known:	Information Known:

Creating with the Story Elements

Directions: Thinking about the story elements of character, setting, and plot in a novel is very important to understanding what is happening and why. Complete **one** of the following activities based on what you've read so far. Be creative and have fun!

Characters

Design and draw dresses that Turtle and Angela Wexler would like to wear. The dresses you design should reflect their personalities and actions. Write brief descriptions of each completed dress.

Setting

Create a map of Sunset Towers. Your map should show where each tenant lives as well as the locations of the restaurant, the coffee shop, and Dr. Wexler's office.

Plot

Create a flow chart showing five to seven major events in the first six chapters.

Vocabulary Overview

Ten key words from this section are provided below with definitions and sentences about how the words are used in the book. Choose one of the vocabulary activity sheets (pages 25 or 26) for students to complete as they read this section. Monitor the students as they work to ensure the definitions they have found are accurate and relate to the text. Finally, discuss these important vocabulary words with the students. If you think these words or other words in the section warrant more time devoted to them, there are suggestions in the introduction for other vocabulary activities (page 5).

Word	Definition	Sentence about Text
jaunty (ch. 7)	cheerful, lively, and self-confident	Sandy McSouthers acts **jaunty** as he gets a chair ready for Judge Ford.
louse (ch. 7)	a person who is unpleasant and disagreeable	Mr. Hoo does not like Sam Westing and thinks he is a **louse** who deserves to die.
buttressed (ch. 8)	held something up	The huge snowdrifts are **buttressed** against the Westing house.
inscrutable (ch. 8)	being hard to understand or mysterious	Madame Hoo is quiet and **inscrutable** to the other tenants.
impeccable (ch. 8)	something or someone who is without fault or error	Even though Sydelle's logic about not being in danger is **impeccable**, Angela is still nervous.
defiantly (ch. 9)	acting in a rebellious manner	Turtle **defiantly** keeps her clues a secret from her mother.
prattling (ch. 10)	going on and on about something unimportant	Grace continues **prattling** on about her relationship to Sam Westing.
chiding (ch. 10)	criticizing a person harshly	Angela is upset with her mother for **chiding** her about her costume in front of the other guests.
coiffure (ch. 10)	hairstyle	Mrs. Wexler wants Angela to change her **coiffure** before the wedding.
larcenist (ch. 11)	a person who steals	Sydelle thinks Grace Wexler has stolen her notes and calls her a **larcenist**.

Name _____

Date _____

Understanding Vocabulary Words

Directions: The following words appear in this section of the book. Use context clues and reference materials to determine an accurate definition for each word.

Word	Definition
jaunty (ch. 7)	
louse (ch. 7)	
buttressed (ch. 8)	
inscrutable (ch. 8)	
impeccable (ch. 8)	
defiantly (ch. 9)	
prattling (ch. 10)	
chiding (ch. 10)	
coiffure (ch. 10)	
larcenist (ch. 11)	

Name _____

Date _____

During-Reading Vocabulary Activity

Directions: As you read these chapters, record at least eight important words on the lines below. Try to find interesting, difficult, intriguing, special, or funny words. Your words can be long or short. They can be hard or easy to spell. After each word, use context clues in the text and reference materials to define the word.

- _____
- _____
- _____
- _____
- _____
- _____
- _____
- _____
- _____
- _____

Directions: Respond to these questions about the words in this section.

1. Why is Turtle **defiantly** refusing to give her mother the clues she and Flora Baumbach have?

   _____

   _____

   _____

2. Give examples of ways Madame Hoo is **inscrutable**.

   _____

   _____

   _____

Analyzing the Literature

Provided below are discussion questions you can use in small groups, with the whole class, or for written assignments. Each question is given at two levels so you can choose the right question for each group of students. Activity sheets with these questions are provided (pages 28–29) if you want students to write their responses. For each question, a few key discussion points are provided for your reference.

Story Element	■ Level 1	▲ Level 2	Key Discussion Points
Character	Think about Angela in the beginning of the book. How is this game starting to change her?	Compare and contrast Angela's personality at the beginning of the book to what she is like now.	At the beginning of the book, Angela seems to just go along with her mother and fiancé's ideas. As the story develops, the reader sees more of Angela's thoughts and doubts. Angela begins to question what she is doing and what she is being told.
Character	What do readers know about Sydelle Pulaski at this point?	What impact does Sydelle Pulaski have on the rest of the players?	Sydelle Pulaski is a secretary who takes shorthand notes of the will. She walks with a crutch and complains of other ailments. Now that she has the sought-after notes and a beautiful partner, she is getting the attention she desires. Other players act in ways that will get them glimpses of her notes.
Setting	What is it like for the snowed-in tenants at Sunset Towers?	Describe the current setting at Sunset Towers and how people are interacting with each other.	Snow keeps the tenants from getting out. They have time to study clues, ask questions, and visit other players. All players are interested in Sydelle's notebook. They are placing notes in the elevator about meeting and having group discussions about their clues. They are getting together socially to solve the mystery.
Plot	How do the players react when the bomb goes off?	In what ways does the bomb present a challenge or danger to the players of the game?	Panic breaks out when they hear the blast from the coffee shop kitchen. When they realize there are no injuries, the heirs debate the cause and what should be done. The players not only have to contend with a murderer, but a bomber as well.

Name _____

Date _____

Analyzing the Literature

Directions: Think about the section you just read. Read each question, and state your response with textual evidence.

1. Think about Angela in the beginning of the book. How is this game starting to change her?

   _____
   _____
   _____
   _____

2. What do we know about Sydelle Pulaski?

   _____
   _____
   _____
   _____

3. What is it like for the snowed in tenants at Sunset Towers?

   _____
   _____
   _____
   _____

4. How do the players react when the bomb goes off?

   _____
   _____
   _____
   _____

Name _____

Date _____

▲ Analyzing the Literature

Directions: Think about the section you just read. Read each question, and state your response with textual evidence.

1. Compare and contrast Angela's personality at the beginning of the book to what she is like now.

    _____

    _____

    _____

    _____

2. What impact does Sydelle Pulaski have on the rest of the players?

    _____

    _____

    _____

    _____

3. Describe the current setting at Sunset Towers and how people are interacting with each other.

    _____

    _____

    _____

    _____

4. In what ways does the bomb present a challenge or danger to the players of the game?

    _____

    _____

    _____

    _____

Name _____

Date _____

Reader Response

Directions: Choose one of the following prompts about this section to answer. Be sure you include a topic sentence in your response, use textual evidence to support your opinion, and provide a strong conclusion that summarizes your opinion.

Writing Prompts

- **Informative/Explanatory Piece**—Turtle is the youngest player in the Westing Game. How do you relate to her, and what advice can you give her about playing the game against others who are older than she is?
- **Opinion/Argument Piece**—The shorthand notes Sydelle Pulaski takes during the reading of the will give her an advantage. What do you think she should do with the notes? Give reasons to support your response.

_____

_____

_____

_____

_____

_____

_____

_____

_____

_____

_____

_____

_____

_____

_____

_____

Name _____

Date _____

Close Reading the Literature

Directions: Closely reread the section in chapter 8 that starts with, "Sydelle was disappointed, 'It is not what you have, it's what you don't have that counts.'" Read until the end of chapter 8. Read each question, and then revisit the text to find evidence that supports your answer.

1. How is the game of chess being used in this story?

    _____

    _____

    _____

2. Describe the implications of Sydelle discovering that her shorthand notebook has been stolen.

    _____

    _____

    _____

    _____

3. What does Sydelle do in the second-to-last paragraph of the chapter? What words does the author use to communicate this information?

    _____

    _____

    _____

    _____

4. Describe Angela's personality in this passage.

    _____

    _____

    _____

    _____

Name _____

Date _____

Making Connections—Moving Pieces

Directions: The heirs are like players in a game as they try to solve the mystery and earn the inheritance. While snowed in at Sunset Towers, they make many different moves as they play the Westing Game. Create a web, flow chart, or diagram that shows where the players are and what they are doing in this section of the book.

Name _____

Date _____

Creating with the Story Elements

Directions: Thinking about the story elements of character, setting, and plot in a novel is very important to understanding what is happening and why. Complete **one** of the following activities based on what you've read so far. Be creative and have fun!

Characters

Chose one character from the book. Write a list of all you know about this character, and draw a picture showing what you think this character looks like. Label any special features in your drawing.

Setting

What would happen if Sunset Towers was not located in Westingtown? Illustrate a new setting for the story, and provide at least a paragraph below the drawing that details how the setting affects the game, players, and clues.

Plot

Judge J. J. Ford does some extra investigating in this section of the book. Summarize what she learns. How might this information help her solve the mystery?

Vocabulary Overview

Ten key words from this section are provided below with definitions and sentences about how the words are used in the book. Choose one of the vocabulary activity sheets (pages 35 or 36) for students to complete as they read this section. Monitor the students as they work to ensure the definitions they have found are accurate and relate to the text. Finally, discuss these important vocabulary words with the students. If you think these words or other words in the section warrant more time devoted to them, there are suggestions in the introduction for other vocabulary activities (page 5).

Word	Definition	Sentence about Text
harried (ch. 13)	bothered by a lot of problems or worries	Mr. Hoo is **harried** by his responsibility in the restaurant and concern about his family.
protruding (ch. 14)	sticking out	Judge Ford sees a container **protruding** from Sandy McSouthers's pocket.
dejectedly (ch. 14)	feeling sad because of a failure or loss	Sandy answers **dejectedly** when he is reminded he came up with too many suspects.
obsequious (ch. 14)	excessively attentive in efforts to win favor from people	Sandy's **obsequious** behavior toward the tenants in Sunset Towers makes him well liked by most.
peevishly (ch. 14)	showing annoyance or irritation	Grace speaks **peevishly** to her partner because she is worried about a gas explosion.
trousseau (ch. 14)	the possessions of a bride, including clothes and household items	Angela stitches an item for her wedding **trousseau** while waiting in the lobby.
despondently (ch. 16)	feeling great sadness or hopelessness	Grace feels helpless and speaks **despondently** when she sees Angela's injuries.
incinerator (ch. 17)	a machine for burning trash	It is thought by the residents of Sunset Towers that another bomb is behind the **incinerator**.
culled (ch. 17)	collected or gathered	Sandy is proud of his notebook and the information he **culled** from the investigator's reports.
malady (ch. 18)	a disorder or disease	Judge Ford is confused by Sydelle's recent **malady** since the report does not show her to have an illness.

Name _____

Date _____

Understanding Vocabulary Words

Directions: The following words appear in this section of the book. Use context clues and reference materials to determine an accurate definition for each word.

Word	Definition
harried (ch. 13)	
protruding (ch. 14)	
dejectedly (ch. 14)	
obsequious (ch. 14)	
peevishly (ch. 14)	
trousseau (ch. 14)	
despondently (ch. 16)	
incinerator (ch. 17)	
culled (ch. 17)	
malady (ch. 18)	

Name _____

Date _____

During-Reading Vocabulary Activity

Directions: As you read these chapters, record at least eight important words on the lines below. Try to find interesting, difficult, intriguing, special, or funny words. Your words can be long or short. They can be hard or easy to spell. After each word, use context clues in the text and reference materials to define the word.

- _____
- _____
- _____
- _____
- _____
- _____
- _____
- _____
- _____
- _____

Directions: Now, organize your words. Rewrite each of your words on a sticky note. Work as a group to create a bar graph of your words. You should stack any words that are the same on top of one another. Different words appear in different columns. Finally, discuss with a group why certain words were chosen more often than other words.

Analyzing the Literature

Provided below are discussion questions you can use in small groups, with the whole class, or for written assignments. Each question is given at two levels so you can choose the right question for each group of students. Activity sheets with these questions are provided (pages 38–39) if you want students to write their responses. For each question, a few key discussion points are provided for your reference.

Story Element	■ Level 1	▲ Level 2	Key Discussion Points
Character	Which of the heirs are not suspected of being bombers? Why?	Do you think the tenants' reasons for not suspecting Chris or Angela of being the bombers are good reasons? Explain your thinking.	Chris is not suspected of being the bomber because Chris is in a wheelchair, and Angela seems to be the perfect daughter and young woman. As we learn more about both, we realize their characters are much more complex.
Setting	Where have the bombs gone off at Sunset Towers?	What is the significance of the timing and locations of the bombs? Do you think the bomber is really trying to hurt people? Explain.	Bombs have gone off in the coffee shop, in the Chinese restaurant, and in the Wexler's apartment. The bombs are set in places where there are a lot of people. Maybe the bomber wants to scare them and see their reactions. The explosions do not seem to be large enough to cause serious injuries.
Character	What does Dr. Denton Deere do that shows a more caring attitude?	Describe the relationship between Dr. Denton Deere and his partner, Chris.	At the beginning, Denton had only been interested in his share of the money. He shows he cares for Angela by bringing in the best plastic surgeon when she is hurt. He makes plans to take Chris to the hospital where a nerve doctor is going to see him. When Chris later offers to sign the check, Denton doesn't want the money.
Plot	How does Grace Wexler seem to start taking over Shin Hoo's Restaurant?	What are the impacts of Grace's seating arrangements at Shin Hoo's Restaurant?	Grace puts a sign in the elevator advertising the restaurant and appoints herself hostess. The heirs are paired at the tables with people they do not know well. As they talk at dinner, they learn more about each other.

Name _____

Date _____

Analyzing the Literature

Directions: Think about the section you just read. Read each question, and state your response with textual evidence.

1. Which of the heirs are not suspected of being bombers? Why?

   _____

   _____

   _____

   _____

2. Where have the bombs gone off at Sunset Towers?

   _____

   _____

   _____

   _____

3. What does Dr. Denton Deere do that shows a more caring attitude?

   _____

   _____

   _____

   _____

4. How does Grace Wexler seem to start taking over Shin Hoo's Restaurant?

   _____

   _____

   _____

   _____

Name _____

Date _____

▲ Analyzing the Literature

Directions: Think about the section you just read. Read each question, and state your response with textual evidence.

1. Do you think the tenant's reasons for not suspecting Chris or Angela of being the bombers are good reasons? Explain your thinking.

   _____

   _____

   _____

   _____

2. What is the significance of the timing and locations of the bombs? Do you think the bomber is really trying to hurt people? Explain.

   _____

   _____

   _____

   _____

3. Describe the relationship between Dr. Denton Deere and his partner, Chris.

   _____

   _____

   _____

   _____

4. What are the impacts of Grace's seating arrangements at Shin Hoo's Restaurant?

   _____

   _____

   _____

   _____

Name _____

Date _____

Reader Response

Directions: Choose one of the following prompts about this section to answer. Be sure you include a topic sentence in your response, use textual evidence to support your opinion, and provide a strong conclusion that summarizes your opinion.

Writing Prompts

- **Opinion/Argument Piece**—Sydelle thinks she knows who the bomber is: her partner Angela. Why does she think this? Should she keep that secret to herself, or should she tell some of the other players or even the police? Explain your reasons.
- **Narrative Piece**—Angela finds a letter in Sydelle's cosmetic bag with the clues "THY" and "BEAUTIFUL" at the bottom. Imagine you were Angela and saw the letter. What conclusions would you come to?

_____

_____

_____

_____

_____

_____

_____

_____

_____

_____

_____

_____

_____

_____

Close Reading the Literature

Directions: Closely reread part of chapter 16 starting with, "Angela glanced at her watch and reached for the tall, thin carton wrapped in gold foil." End where Theo and Chris discuss whether or not Crow was in the building when the first two bombs went off. Read each question, and then revisit the text to find evidence that supports your answer.

1. Using evidence from the text, what inference does the author want you to make from the sentence where Crow mutters, "Her blessed Angela was almost killed"?

   _____

   _____

   _____

2. Summarize the sequence of events that unfold in this passage. Why is this order of events important to the overall story, and how does it relate to the other bombings?

   _____

   _____

   _____

3. What do we learn about Angela from this text? What can we infer about her?

   _____

   _____

   _____

4. What new details does the author present in this text? How do these ideas help the reader play along in the Westing game?

   _____

   _____

   _____

Name _____

Date _____

Making Connections—
Writing Questions to the Author

Directions: The author, Ellen Raskin, adds mystery and detail to this story leaving the reader with a lot of questions. Pretend you have an opportunity to ask Raskin some of the questions you have about the book. Create a list of questions using the following stems. Your questions should relate to the events that take place in chapters 13–18.

Stem to Use	Your Question
What?	
How?	
Why?	
Who?	
I wonder...	

Now, imagine you are Ellen Raskin. How would you respond to your questions? Choose one question from above, and write a response to it. Use the lines below to give a complete response to your favorite question.

_____

_____

_____

_____

Name _____

Date _____

Creating with the Story Elements

Directions: Thinking about the story elements of character, setting, and plot in a novel is very important to understanding what is happening and why. Complete **one** of the following activities based on what you've read so far. Be creative and have fun!

Characters

Think about Turtle's personality. Create a web graphic organizer with Turtle's name in the middle. Write four character traits that describe Turtle in the circles around her name. For each trait, give an example how Turtle's relationship with another player is affected by that particular character trait.

Setting

Doug follows Otis Amber around town at the request of his partner, Theo. Create a map of the places Otis goes. Label locations on the map. Use numbered arrows to show the order of his travel, and record the number of miles between stops.

Plot

There have been many facts and opinions (or gossip) introduced in this section of the book. Create a T-chart labeled *Fact* and *Gossip*. Record the facts and gossip you find in this section of the book.

Vocabulary Overview

Ten key words from this section are provided below with definitions and sentences about how the words are used in the book. Choose one of the vocabulary activity sheets (pages 45 or 46) for students to complete as they read this section. Monitor the students as they work to ensure the definitions they have found are accurate and relate to the text. Finally, discuss these important vocabulary words with the students. If you think these words or other words in the section warrant more time devoted to them, there are suggestions in the introduction for other vocabulary activities (page 5).

Word	Definition	Sentence about Text
penance (ch. 19)	the act of doing a good deed to make up for past wrongs	Berthe Crow's **penance** for a past wrong is having to return to the Westing house.
covetousness (ch. 19)	extreme desire for other's material things	Berthe Crow views Grace Wexler's desire for money and possessions as **covetousness**.
derelicts (ch. 21)	persons without a home, job, or property	Doug sees **derelicts** at the soup kitchen as he spies on Otis Amber.
meticulous (ch. 21)	extra attention to detail	Sandy McSouthers is showing **meticulous** detail to the notes he writes.
delinquent (ch. 21)	a young person who regularly does things that are illegal	The heirs think of Turtle as a **delinquent** when they come to believe she is the bomber.
pompous (ch. 22)	arrogant or conceited	Dr. Denton Deere realizes that he spoke in a **pompous** manner to Chris.
ornithologist (ch. 23)	a person who studies birds	Chris pictures himself as an **ornithologist** after he assumes his brother wrote that title next to his name.
tittered (ch. 23)	laughed nervously	Grace Wexler falls to the floor, and the players **titter** at her unsteadiness.
derisive (ch. 23)	expressing ridicule; mocking someone or something	The heirs' **derisive** smiles disappear when they realize Sydelle's song includes their clues.
writhing (ch. 24)	moving in a rolling or twisting motion	Sandy McSouthers falls to the ground and begins **writhing** as the doctors rush to help.

Name _____

Date _____

Understanding Vocabulary Words

Directions: The following words appear in this section of the book. Use context clues and reference materials to determine an accurate definition for each word.

Word	Definition
penance (ch. 19)	
covetousness (ch. 19)	
derelicts (ch. 21)	
meticulous (ch. 21)	
delinquent (ch. 21)	
pompous (ch. 22)	
ornithologist (ch. 23)	
tittered (ch. 23)	
derisive (ch. 23)	
writhing (ch. 24)	

Name _____

Date _____

During-Reading Vocabulary Activity

Directions: As you read these chapters, record at least eight important words on the lines below. Try to find interesting, difficult, intriguing, special, or funny words. Your words can be long or short. They can be hard or easy to spell. After each word, use context clues in the text and reference materials to define the word.

- _____
- _____
- _____
- _____
- _____
- _____
- _____
- _____
- _____
- _____

Directions: Respond to these questions about the words in this section.

1. Why is Sandy McSouthers **writhing** in pain on the floor of Sam Westing's house?

_____

_____

_____

2. Give examples of Grace Wexler's **covetousness**.

_____

_____

_____

Analyzing the Literature

Provided below are discussion questions you can use in small groups, with the whole class, or for written assignments. Each question is given at two levels so you can choose the right question for each group of students. Activity sheets with these questions are provided (pages 48–49) if you want students to write their responses. For each question, a few key discussion points are provided for your reference.

Story Element	■ Level 1	▲ Level 2	Key Discussion Points
Plot	What does Judge Ford learn from her private investigator about who the killer might be?	How does thinking she knows the identity of the killer change the game for Judge Ford?	The information leads Judge Ford to believe that Berthe Crow, Westing's ex-wife, is being framed for his murder. The Judge now feels she must protect Crow, as she may be in danger.
Character	Who is Berthe Erica Crow?	What do Berthe Crow's religious rants and note droppings have to do with her guilty conscience?	Berthe Crow is the ex-wife of Sam Westing. Their daughter Violet took her own life rather than marry for money as her mother had insisted. Crow uses religion as a way to repent because she believes she caused her daughter's death. Angela, Denton, and Theo seem to parallel her daughter's relationships, so she tries to bring the right ones together.
Plot	Who confesses to being the bomber? How is that person discovered?	Why does Turtle allow herself to be caught as the bomber? Who is she protecting?	Turtle is found near the elevator the fireworks came out of. A note stating "the bomber strikes again" written on the back of her paper is in the elevator. She is protecting her sister. Turtle believes Angela set the fireworks because of something she saw in Angela's purse.
Character	Why does Grace Wexler change her name?	Grace Wexler is secretive about her name. What other secrets does she keep?	She changes her name from Grace Windkloppel because she is ashamed of her family and connection to the cleaning lady. She is unhappy with her own life and wants more for Angela than the life she has. She believes Turtle was switched at birth.

Name _____

Date _____

Analyzing the Literature

Directions: Think about the section you just read. Read each question, and state your response with textual evidence.

1. What does Judge Ford learn from her private investigator about who the killer might be?

_____

_____

_____

_____

2. Who is Berthe Erica Crow?

_____

_____

_____

_____

3. Who confesses to being the bomber? How is that person discovered?

_____

_____

_____

_____

_____

4. Why does Grace Wexler change her name?

_____

_____

_____

_____

Name _____

Date _____

▲ Analyzing the Literature

Directions: Think about the section you just read. Read each question, and state your response with textual evidence.

1. How does thinking she knows the identity of the killer change the game for Judge Ford?

_____

_____

_____

_____

2. What do Berthe Crow's religious rants and note droppings have to do with her guilty conscience?

_____

_____

_____

_____

3. Why does Turtle allow herself to be caught as the bomber? Who is she protecting?

_____

_____

_____

_____

4. Grace Wexler is secretive about her name. What other secrets does she keep?

_____

_____

_____

_____

Name _____

Date _____

Reader Response

Directions: Choose one of the following prompts about this section to answer. Be sure you include a topic sentence in your response, use textual evidence to support your opinion, and provide a strong conclusion that summarizes your opinion.

Writing Prompts

- **Informative/Explanatory Piece**—Based on what you know at this point, who do you think killed Sam Westing? Tell who you think the murderer is, and explain what is leading you to that conclusion.
- **Opinion/Argument Piece**—Turtle confesses to being the bomber even though she is not. She does this to protect her sister. What would you do if you were Turtle? Provide reasons as to why you would or would not confess.

_____

_____

_____

_____

_____

_____

_____

_____

_____

_____

_____

_____

_____

_____

_____

_____

Name _____

Date _____

Close Reading the Literature

Directions: Closely reread the paragraph toward the beginning of chapter 24 that starts with, "Madame Hoo knew from the shifting eyes that a bad person was in the room." Stop reading at the sentence that states, "The heirs heard a low groan, then a rasping rattle…then nothing." Read each question, and then revisit the text to find evidence that supports your answer.

1. Use the text to explain the connection between Sandy McSouthers and Sam Westing. How does Judge Ford make that connection?

   _____

   _____

   _____

   _____

2. What important details in this passage help solve the murder?

   _____

   _____

   _____

   _____

3. What is learned about Madame Hoo in the beginning of this passage? What words does the author use to communicate this information?

   _____

   _____

   _____

4. How does Sandy McSouthers try to move the players towards solving the mystery? Cite reasons from the text that hint at why he might be trying to help.

   _____

   _____

   _____

Name _____

Date _____

Making Connections—Truth or Lies?

Directions: There are many truths and lies told and confessed during the Westing Game. Determine if each statement is a truth or lie, and complete the second column. Give evidence to support your answer. Add two more statements to the chart. Ask a classmate to determine if your statements are truths or lies and provide evidence to support their responses. When they finish, have a discussion about the truths and lies.

Statement	Truth or Lie	Evidence
Sam Westing is alive.		
Berthe Crow is Mrs. Westing.		

Name _____

Date _____

Creating with the Story Elements

Directions: Thinking about the story elements of character, setting, and plot in a novel is very important to understanding what is happening and why. Complete **one** of the following activities based on what you've read so far. Be creative and have fun!

Characters

Create sketches of what Sam Westing looked like 15 years ago and what he (Sandy McSouthers) looks like now. List reasons for his change in appearance below your sketches.

Setting

Sunset Towers is the location of many unusual events. Pretend you are the writer of the apartment newsletter. Make a list of topics you would include in your newsletter from this section of the book.

Plot

Who did it? Create a three column chart to help figure out who did what. Label the columns: Question, Heir/Heiress, and Evidence. Fill the first column with questions such as *Who is the "murderer"?* or *Who is not supposed to be an heir?* Complete the rest of the chart to answer each question.

Teacher Plans

Vocabulary Overview

Ten key words from this section are provided below with definitions and sentences about how the words are used in the book. Choose one of the vocabulary activity sheets (pages 55 or 56) for students to complete as they read this section. Monitor the students as they work to ensure the definitions they have found are accurate and relate to the text. Finally, discuss these important vocabulary words with the students. If you think these words or other words in the section warrant more time devoted to them, there are suggestions in the introduction for other vocabulary activities (page 5).

Word	Definition	Sentence about Text
stoolie (ch. 25)	someone acting as an informer for the police	Mr. Hoo is relieved not to be the **stoolie** responsible for Berthe's arrest.
inherit (ch. 25)	to receive something from someone after death	The heirs work to determine why Crow would **inherit** the money.
presided (ch. 26)	acted as a leader	Judge Ford declares the Westing Game court to be the lowest she has **presided** over.
tousled (ch. 26)	to make someone's hair messy	Otis Amber's hair looks **tousled**.
bristled (ch. 26)	to show signs of anger	When Judge Ford realizes her great mistake in not investigating Sandy McSouthers, she **bristles**.
embalmed (ch. 26)	a way of preserving a dead body	While under oath, Denton Deere states Samuel Westing's body was **embalmed**.
benefactor (ch. 26)	someone who helps by giving money	The players say a silent prayer for their **benefactor**, Samuel Westing.
discontented (ch. 27)	not happy	The heirs let out a **discontented** grumble when they realize they will not receive the money.
smother (ch. 28)	to stifle or suppress	Not wanting to demand too much from Chris, Judge Ford promises to write rather than visit so she won't **smother** him.
stouter (ch. 29)	to be sturdy and strong	In his new job, Mr. Hoo looks happier and **stouter**.

Name _____

Date _____

Understanding Vocabulary Words

Directions: The following words appear in this section of the book. Use context clues and reference materials to determine an accurate definition for each word.

Word	Definition
stoolie (ch. 25)	
inherit (ch. 25)	
presided (ch. 26)	
tousled (ch. 26)	
bristled (ch. 26)	
embalmed (ch. 26)	
benefactor (ch. 26)	
discontented (ch. 27)	
smother (ch. 28)	
stouter (ch. 29)	

Name _____

Date _____

During-Reading Vocabulary Activity

Directions: As you read these chapters, choose five important words from the story. Then, use those five words to complete this word flow chart. On each arrow, write a vocabulary word. In the boxes between the words, explain how the words connect. An example for the words *discontented* and *inherit* has been done for you.

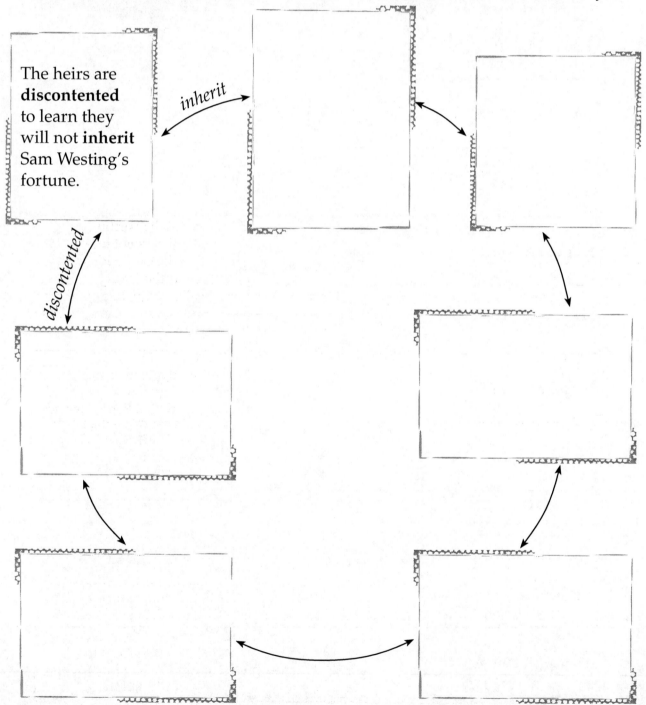

The heirs are **discontented** to learn they will not **inherit** Sam Westing's fortune.

inherit

discontented

Analyzing the Literature

Provided below are discussion questions you can use in small groups, with the whole class, or for written assignments. Each question is given at two levels so you can choose the right question for each group of students. Activity sheets with these questions are provided (pages 58–59) if you want students to write their responses. For each question, a few key discussion points are provided for your reference.

Story Element	■ Level 1	▲ Level 2	Key Discussion Points
Plot	Who wins the inheritance, and how?	How does the inheritance change or affect the players in the game?	Turtle wins the inheritance. She figures out what Sam meant in the will regarding *fourth*. The other players realize many of their dreams after the game ends. They get married, go to college, change jobs, and find great success in life.
Character	Who is Julian R. Eastman?	What connections can be made between Julian R. Eastman and Sam Westing?	Julian Eastman was named chief executive officer of the Westing corporation after Sam went into hiding following the car accident. Eastman is the fourth identity of Sam Westing. His name, Eastman, completes the north, south, and west connection to Sam's aliases.
Character	Who is Otis Amber?	In what ways throughout the story has Otis helped or hindered the players in the game?	Otis Amber is a private investigator working as a delivery boy. He is hired by Sam Westing and J. J. Ford. He uses his connections to get Crow the job at Sunset Towers. He tells Turtle a story that leads her into the Westing house the night of the murder.
Setting	Describe what leads up to the burning of the Westing house.	What is the symbolism between the Westing house burning and the conclusion of the game?	Turtle is able to use Sam's clue about the Fourth of July and the evidence that Sandy is Sam to determine he will set off fireworks using her candle. The Westing house burns down the evening Turtle and the Judge solve most of the Westing Game. The home burns to symbolize the end of the Westing estate and an end to the game.

Name _____

Date _____

Analyzing the Literature

Directions: Think about the section you just read. Read each question, and state your response with textual evidence.

1. Who wins the inheritance, and how?

_____

_____

_____

_____

_____

2. Who is Julian R. Eastman?

_____

_____

_____

_____

3. Who is Otis Amber?

_____

_____

_____

_____

4. Describe what leads up to the burning of the Westing mansion.

_____

_____

_____

_____

Name _____

Date _____

▲ Analyzing the Literature

Directions: Think about the section you just read. Read each question, and state your response with textual evidence.

1. How does the inheritance change or affect the players in the game?

   _____

   _____

   _____

   _____

2. What connections can be made between Julian R. Eastman and Sam Westing?

   _____

   _____

   _____

   _____

3. In what ways throughout the story has Otis helped or hindered the players in the game?

   _____

   _____

   _____

   _____

4. What is the symbolism between the Westing mansion burning and the conclusion of the game?

   _____

   _____

   _____

   _____

Name _____

Date _____

Reader Response

Directions: Choose one of the following prompts about this section to answer. Be sure you include a topic sentence in your response, use textual evidence to support your opinion, and provide a strong conclusion that summarizes your opinion.

Writing Prompts

- **Narrative Piece**—Angela becomes a completely different person during the Westing Game. How does the game change her for the better?
- **Informative/Explanatory Piece**—Explain the gift of education as seen in this section. Who gives, and who receives?

_____

_____

_____

_____

_____

_____

_____

_____

_____

_____

_____

_____

_____

_____

_____

_____

Name _____

Date _____

Close Reading the Literature

Directions: Closely reread the section that starts with, "One half hour to go," and continue reading to the end of chapter 26. Read each question, and then revisit the text to find evidence that supports your answer.

1. What does the author want you to infer from the sentence, "Turtle surveyed her stupefied audience. Good, they bought her little fib"? What evidence from the text helps you to make that inference?

   _____
   _____
   _____
   _____

2. What details can you identify from this text that describe how similar Turtle is to her great-uncle Sam? How do these details influence your feelings about Turtle?

   _____
   _____
   _____

3. What helpful information does the author provide about Sam Westing in this text?

   _____
   _____
   _____

4. How do these events make the players believe the mystery of Sam Westing's death is solved? Provide examples from the text.

   _____
   _____
   _____

Name _____

Date _____

Making Connections—A Man of Many Disguises

Directions: Sam Westing uses three other names for himself throughout the story. Write each of his names in one of the bubbles below. Then, in each bubble, give details about the role he plays with each alias.

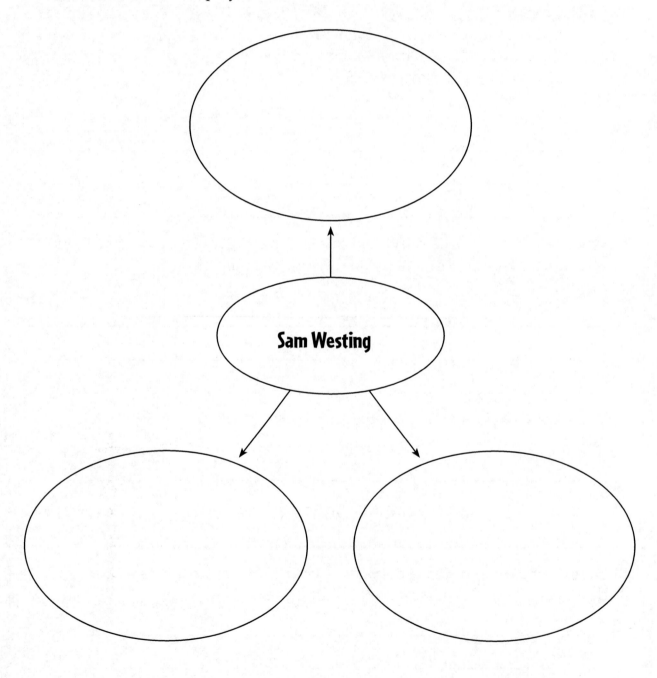

Name _____

Date _____

Creating with the Story Elements

Directions: Thinking about the story elements of character, setting, and plot in a novel is very important to understanding what is happening and why. Complete **one** of the following activities based on what you've read so far. Be creative and have fun!

Characters

Imagine you have an opportunity to interview one of the characters from the story. Choose a character to interview. Write a list of five questions for your character. Then, answer your questions in the way your interviewee might respond.

Setting

Create a drawing to show what the "courtroom" in Judge Ford's apartment looks like. Include a caption that explains what is happening in the drawing.

Plot

Draw a comic strip version of chapter 28, "Five Years Pass." Be sure to include information that details where each player of the game is five years later.

Name _____

Date _____

Post-Reading Theme Thoughts

Directions: Read each of the statements in the first column. Choose a main character from *The Westing Game*. Think about that character's point of view. From that character's perspective, decide if the character would agree or disagree with the statements. Record the character's opinion by marking an *X* in Agree or Disagree for each statement. Explain your choices in the third column using text evidence.

Character I Chose: _____

Statement	Agree	Disagree	Explain Your Answer
Everything isn't always as it seems.			
A chain of events can blow you completely off course.			
Not all conclusions end the way you think they should.			
Sometimes the answer is right there in plain sight.			

Name _____

Date _____

Culminating Activity:
Clues, Clues, Clues

Directions: Clues are given out throughout this book. Not only are they distributed to players on Westing's paper towels as the game begins, but Sandy McSouthers also provides information and ideas to help move the game along. On each paper towel below, provide an example of how Sandy gives hints and clues to help players solve the mysterious Westing Game. Give a page number telling where you find each example.

Name _____

Date _____

Culminating Activity:
Clues, Clues, Clues (cont.)

Directions: When your graphic organizer is complete and you have a greater understanding of the Westing Game, select **one** of the culminating projects below to complete.

Reader's Theater

Write a reader's theater script that shows a character using the clues provided by Sandy McSouthers to make progress in solving the mystery. Make copies of your script, and have other students join you perform it for the class.

New Ending

Turtle uses the clues to win the game, keep a secret, and become extremely wealthy. If Turtle had not followed the clues and won, who might have won? Select a new winner, and outline an ending to the book that tells what would have happened if your character had won.

Matching Game

Use the clues given by Sandy McSouthers through the book to make a matching game for your classmates. List each of the clues on a piece of paper towel. On different pieces of paper towel, list how each clue helps solve the mystery. Have friends match the paper towels with clues to the paper towels that list the solutions to the mystery.

Name _____

Date _____

Comprehension Assessment

Directions: Circle the letter for the best response to each question.

1. Which sentence from the story best explains that Angela finally feels she is able to do things on her own?

   A. "'How about you, Angela, what do you want?' He knew her unspoken answer was, 'I don't know.'"

   B. "These were her mother's friends and the newly married daughters of her mother's friends."

   C. "Blood oozed from an angry gash on her cheek and trickled down her beautiful face."

   D. "They had not asked how she got home from the hospital (by taxi), they had not asked if she was still in pain (not much)…"

2. How does Sydelle Pulaski mistakenly become a player in the Westing Game?

   A. She makes an appointment with Barney Northrup to see an apartment.

   B. There is a slight difference in her first name and the name of Sybil Pulaski.

   C. Sam Westing adds her to the players list to try and throw off the others as they look for clues.

   D. She lies about who she is to those living in Sunset Towers, and they believe her to be a half-sister of Sam Westing.

3. What is the purpose of the song, "America the Beautiful", in this book?

   A. to give Sydelle Pulaski an opportunity to sing in front of people

   B. to give more information about where other clues can be found

   C. to help bring to light the name of the murderer

   D. to remind the players of Sam Westing's great love for America

4. Which detail from the book supports the answer to question number 3?

   E. "'The missing words,' Sydelle Pulaski announced, 'are *ber*, *the*, *erica*, and *crow*. *Berthe Erica Crow!*'"

   F. "She hummed into a pitch pipe and began to sing one note above the pitch she played."

   G. "So take stock in America…and sing in praise of this generous land."

   H. "'Happy Fourth of July,' Turtle shouted as the first rockets lit up the Westing house, lit up the sky.'"

Comprehension Assessment (cont.)

5. Choose words that describe Berthe Crow based on the evidence from the story. There is more than one choice.

   A. reckless

   B. religious

   C. afraid

   D. observant

6. Find and write two details from the text that support your responses to question 5.

   _____

   _____

   _____

   _____

   _____

   _____

7. What are two similarities between Sam Westing and Turtle "T. R." Wexler?

   _____

   _____

   _____

   _____

   _____

   _____

8. Number the events in the order in which they happened.

   _____ Angela keeps the package from exploding onto her sister.

   _____ The players sit at the table and wait for their first clue.

   _____ James Hoo slams Sydelle's notebook down on the table.

   _____ Sam Westing dies peacefully in his home with Turtle nearby.

   _____ Berthe Crow pulls Theo into her apartment and prays with him.

Name _____

Date _____

Response to Literature: Revenge?

Overview: *The Westing Game* is not just a simple game of who-done-it.

- The game is played, a "murderer" is sought, and lives are forever changed because of revenge Sam Westing wants for his daughter's death, brought on by his ex-wife.
- Sam pre-determines not to get back at Crow, his ex-wife, himself, but instead uses others (who do not know they are playing that part) to seek and get revenge.
- Because of the Westing Game, all the players go on to lead lives they may have been unable to lead, had it not been for their role in the game.

Directions: Think about these questions:

1. Why did Sam Westing decide to play such an elaborate game to have Berthe Crow pay for the role she played in their daughter's death?

2. Think about a few players in the game and how their lives turned out. Would they have turned out that way had it not been for the game? Be sure to use specific examples in your answer.

3. Choose three players. How did each player contribute to solving the mystery?

Write an essay based on the answers to the preceding questions. Be sure to include evidence from the text. Your essay should follow these guidelines:

- State a clear opinion.
- Be at least 750 words in length.
- Include answers to all questions asked.
- Draw, directly or indirectly, from *The Westing Game.*
- Provide a conclusion that summarizes your point of view.

Name _____

Date _____

Response to Literature Rubric

Directions: Use this rubric to evaluate student responses.

	Exceptional Writing	Quality Writing	Developing Writing
Focus and Organization	☐ States a clear opinion and elaborates well. Engages readers from the opening hook through the middle to the conclusion. Demonstrates clear understanding of the intended audience and purpose of the piece.	☐ Provides a clear and consistent opinion. Maintains a clear perspective and supports it through elaborating details. Makes the opinion clear in the opening hook and summarizes well in the conclusion.	☐ Provides an inconsistent point of view. Does not support the topic adequately or misses pertinent information. Lacks clarity in the beginning, middle, and conclusion.
Text Evidence	☐ Provides comprehensive and accurate support. Includes relevant and worthwhile text references.	☐ Provides limited support. Provides few supporting text references.	☐ Provides very limited support for the text. Provides no supporting text references.
Written Expression	☐ Uses descriptive and precise language with clarity and intention. Maintains a consistent voice and uses an appropriate tone that supports meaning. Uses multiple sentence types and transitions well between ideas.	☐ Uses a broad vocabulary. Maintains a consistent voice and supports a tone and feelings through language. Varies sentence length and word choices.	☐ Uses a limited and unvaried vocabulary. Provides an inconsistent or weak voice and tone. Provides little to no variation in sentence type and length.
Language Conventions	☐ Capitalizes, punctuates, and spells accurately. Demonstrates complete thoughts within sentences, with accurate subject-verb agreement. Uses paragraphs appropriately and with clear purpose.	☐ Capitalizes, punctuates, and spells accurately. Demonstrates complete thoughts within sentences and appropriate grammar. Paragraphs are properly divided and supported.	☐ Incorrectly capitalizes, punctuates, and spells. Uses fragmented or run-on sentences. Utilizes poor grammar overall. Paragraphs are poorly divided and developed.

The responses provided here are just examples of what the students may answer. Many accurate responses are possible for many questions throughout this unit.

During-Reading Vocabulary Activity—Section 1: Chapters 1–6 (page 16)

1. Crow is putting on a **facade** to hide how she truly feels about the medical procedure being done on her foot.

2. Sam Westing is **eccentric** because he disappears from view and hires a young, unknown attorney to read and carry out his unusual will.

Close Reading the Literature—Section 1: Chapters 1–6 (page 21)

1. When it introduces Sydelle Pulaski, the book says that not everyone is as overjoyed as Grace Windsor Wexler. Sydelle is not excited about the view from her apartment, and she wants to think about moving in rather than taking the apartment immediately.

2. The purpose is to give information about the characters in the game, without naming them. Knowing that there is a burglar, bookie, bomber, and a mistake, helps foreshadow future events at Sunset Towers.

3. Barney Northrup is the name of the real-estate agent for Sunset Towers. His role is to rent out the Sunset Towers apartments to specific people. While we do not know much about him, we can infer that he is a good salesman.

4. The Wexlers rent the apartment even though Mr. Wexler seems less enthusiastic. Grace Wexler is making plans for the furniture and her stationary without discussing the details with her husband.

Making Connections—Section 1: Chapters 1–6 (page 22)

2C: Flora Baumbach—dressmaker

2D: Theodorakis family—Mr. and Mrs. Theodorakis, not invited to the reading of the will; Theo, high school senior, track star; Chris, fifteen, bird watcher, uses a wheelchair

3C: Sydelle Pulaski—a secretary, unnoticed by others

3D: Wexler family—Jake, a doctor; Grace, the wife; Angela, oldest daughter, engaged to Dr. Deere; and Turtle, junior high girl, kicks people who touch her braid

4C: Hoo family—Mr. Hoo, runs restaurant: Mrs. Hoo, longs for China; Doug, son, high school senior

4D: J.J. Ford—first black woman to be elected as judge in the state

During-Reading Vocabulary Activity—Section 2: Chapters 7–12 (page 26)

1. Turtle knows that her mother is only being sweet to her because she wants the clues. So, she **defiantly** refuses to give them to her out of spite.

2. Madame Hoo is described as **inscrutable** because she is so quiet. Others think she does not speak English, so most people do not try to get to know her.

Close Reading the Literature—Section 2: Chapters 7–12 (page 31)

1. Pulaski makes a connection between Theo looking for a chess partner and the obituary, which states Sam Westing was an avid chess player. Angela notices that the judge refers to herself as a pawn, that Otis says he's the king, and Crow is a queen.

2. Sydelle knows that someone was able to get into her apartment. With the shorthand account of the will missing, Sydelle does not have a means of getting people to seek her out.

3. After finding her apartment door open, Sydelle shows that she does not really need to use a crutch. The author uses the words, "Sydelle ran through the apartment with her crutch in the air."

4. Angela seems to be gaining confidence as she works with Sydelle to solve the puzzle. Angela puts clues together and has some good ideas. She still appears timid, especially as she glances in both directions before going into the hallway.

Close Reading the Literature—Section 3: Chapters 13–18 (page 41)

1. Crow holds a special place for Angela in her heart. You can infer that she sees Angela as someone who should be protected.

2. Angela reaches for the thin carton, starts to open it slowly, jerks it away from an impatient Turtle, and the bomb goes off. Angela seems to be protecting Turtle from the bomb in the box. Nobody is seriously injured, and fireworks appear to come from the bomb.

3. Angela seems nervous. After the explosion, Angela does not say anything about her injuries. It could be inferred that she is nervous about her upcoming marriage.

4. Many of the heirs/heiresses could be the potential bomber. Specific information and clues are given about several of the heirs. As readers learn more clues about each player, they are better able to solve the mystery.

During-Reading Vocabulary Activity—Section 4: Chapters 19–24 (page 46)

1. Sandy McSouthers is suffering from some sort of an attack which causes him to be **writhing** in pain. Dr. Sikes enters and declares Sandy dead.

2. Grace Wexler's **covetousness** can be seen in the way she likes to show off. She gets her makeup, hair, and nails done and designs her house and the Hoo's restaurant as showpieces.

Close Reading the Literature—Section 4: Chapters 19–24 (page 51)

1. Judge Ford determines that Sandy McSouthers is Sam Westing. She uses the information about Westing's car accident and McSouthers' battered face to make the connection. The Judge realizes McSouthers is the perfect partner to keep her from learning the truth.

2. Jake reminds everyone that it's what they don't have that is important. This leads the players to put their clues together and find the name Berthe Erica Crow from the missing words in the song. As the clues are being collected, the Judge makes the connection between McSouthers and Westing.

3. Madame Hoo is the burglar. She steals items to sell them and use the money to get back to China. The author says, "She was the bad person." "The crutch lady had her writing-book back," "All those pretty things she was going to sell." and "She would be punished" to help the reader learn more of Madame Hoo's thoughts and actions.

4. After listening to everyone discuss the clues, Sandy suggests arranging the clues to see what is missing. He collects everyone's clues and asks Turtle to write hers again. While he is doing this, he coughs and speaks with a hoarse voice. Maybe knowing he is close to his death makes him want to keep the game going.

Close Reading the Literature—Section 5: Chapters 25–30 (page 61)

1. The author wants the reader to infer that Turtle knows something more than she is telling. The author tells that Turtle didn't taste whisky in the flask.

2. Judge Ford describes the similarity of Turtle's expression when she's winning the case to how Sam Westing's face used to look right before he won a game.

3. Sam Westing has many aliases. He is not only known as Sandy McSouthers, but also Windy Windkloppel (his true name), and Barney Northrup.

4. The players believe the mystery is solved when they name Crow as the answer to the riddle. Turtle convinces them that Sam Westing is Sandy McSouthers, and the game is over. Turtle knows Sam Westing's fourth alias and uses that information to track him down and receive the inheritance.

Making Connections—Section 5: Chapters 25–30 (page 62)

Sam Westing, Sandy McSouthers, Barney Northrup, and Julius R. Eastman

Comprehension Assessment (pages 67–68)

1. D. "They had not asked how she got home from the hospital (by taxi), they had not asked if she was still in pain (not much)…"

2. B. There is a slight difference in her first name and the name of Sybil Pulaski.

3. C. It helps bring to light the name of the murderer.

4. E. "'The missing words,' Sydelle Pulaski announced, 'are ber, the, erica, and crow. Berthe Erica Crow!'"

5. B. religious; C. afraid

6. Examples include: *We are sinners, yet shall we be saved. Let us pray for deliverance, then you must go to your angel, take her away.* and *Somebody's in real danger, Otis, and I think it's me.*

7. Two similarities: Sam is Turtle's great-uncle. They both have similar facial expressions when they know something. Sam and Turtle work smart, not hard.

8. 3, 1, 2, 5, 4